# Glucose Goddess
## *Cookbook*

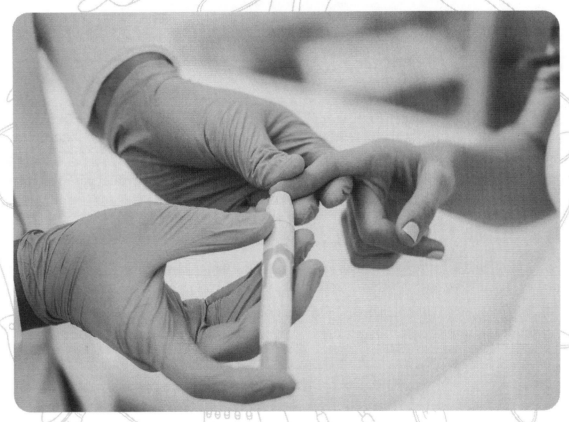

**100 Easy Low-Sugar Recipes for Health and Vitality to Enhance Your Wellbeing and Longevity Through Smart Diet and Blood Sugar Control**

# Alice M.Smith

**Copyright © 2023**

**Alice M. Smith**

**DISCLAIMER**

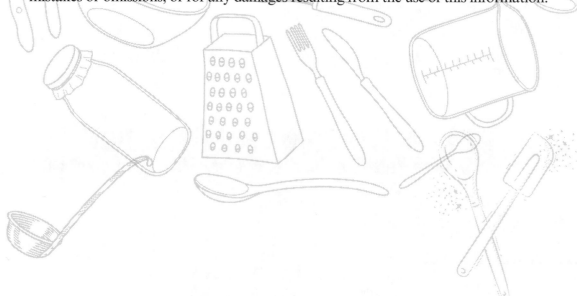

# TABLE OF CONTENTS

# ABOUT THE BOOK

TThe "Glucose Goddess Cookbook: Blood Sugar Control" is your one-stop shop for delectable, healthful meals that help regulate blood sugar levels while pleasing your taste buds. This cookbook is jam-packed with simple recipes and helpful hints to make healthy eating a pleasurable and uncomplicated experience.

Discover a treasure trove of delectable recipes designed expressly to promote blood sugar stability. From vivid salads to robust main courses and delectable desserts, each recipe is carefully designed to balance nutrition without sacrificing taste. This guidebook appeals to both novice and seasoned cooks, with straightforward directions and easily accessible supplies.

Accept a varied selection of culinary creations that highlight elements believed to improve blood sugar management. Whether you have diabetes or simply want to eat a more balanced diet, this cookbook will help you enjoy a variety of recipes without worry or compromising flavor.

The "Glucose Goddess Cookbook" is more than simply a collection of recipes; it's a tool for cultivating a healthy relationship with food. Take control of your health one tasty dish at a time with this vital guide to maintaining balanced blood sugar levels via delectable meals.

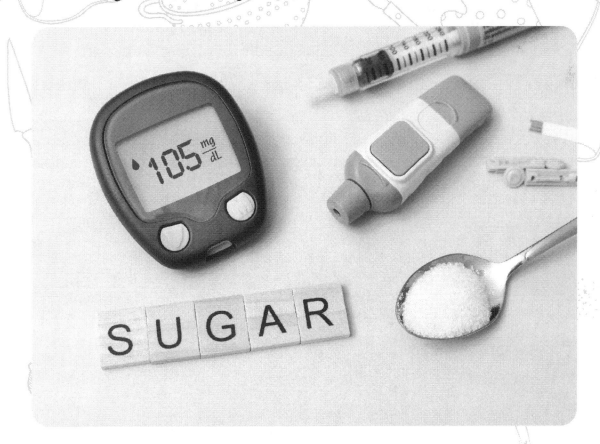

# INTRODUCTION

Welcome to the Glucose Goddess Cookbook, a wonderful, healthful culinary adventure meant to equip you with the expertise of maintaining regulated blood sugar levels. This cookbook is your trusty friend on this tasty journey, whether you're looking for methods to enhance your health or strategies to control your blood sugar.

Understanding the importance of blood sugar regulation is critical for general health. Blood glucose fluctuations can have an influence on energy, mood, and long-term health. But don't worry! This cookbook isn't about restriction or dull meals; it's about celebrating wonderful, healthy cuisine that supports glucose stability in your body.

Here, we begin on a journey that balances taste and health, providing a wealth of recipes meticulously picked to help you manage your blood sugar without sacrificing flavor. From vivid salads to hearty main courses and delectable desserts, each meal is created with simplicity and conscious ingredients, keeping your health objectives in mind.

You'll find a treasure mine of culinary inspiration here, appealing to a wide range of tastes, preferences, and dietary requirements. Whether you're a seasoned chef or a newbie in the kitchen, these recipes are designed to be approachable and simple to prepare, enabling you to discover the delights of cooking while prioritizing your health.

Furthermore, this cookbook is more than just a collection of recipes; it is a thorough reference. We've weaved in key suggestions, nutritional insights, and practical guidance from experts to provide you with the knowledge you need to make smart food and lifestyle decisions. By utilizing this resource, you will not only learn to prepare delectable meals, but you will also receive useful insights on effectively maintaining steady blood sugar levels.

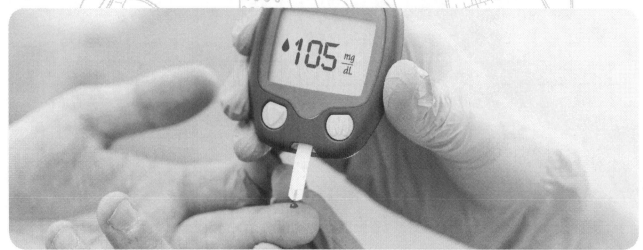

Our goal is to dispel the myth that healthy eating is equated with blandness. Instead, we ask you to experience the rich tastes, textures, and fragrances provided by each dish in this volume. By adopting the Glucose Goddess mindset, you will have a harmonious connection with food—one that feeds your body while tantalizing your taste senses.

As you read through these pages, keep in mind that this cookbook is a transformational tool—a catalyst for embracing a lifestyle that promotes balance, wellness, and, most importantly, enjoyment. These dishes will take you on a gourmet journey that will not only satisfy your appetite but will also nourish your health.

So join us on this fascinating culinary adventure, and let the Glucose Goddess Cookbook help you to mastering blood sugar management while enjoying every mouthful along the way. Cheers to a journey full of delectable tastes, bright health, and the delight of taking control of your blood sugar destiny.

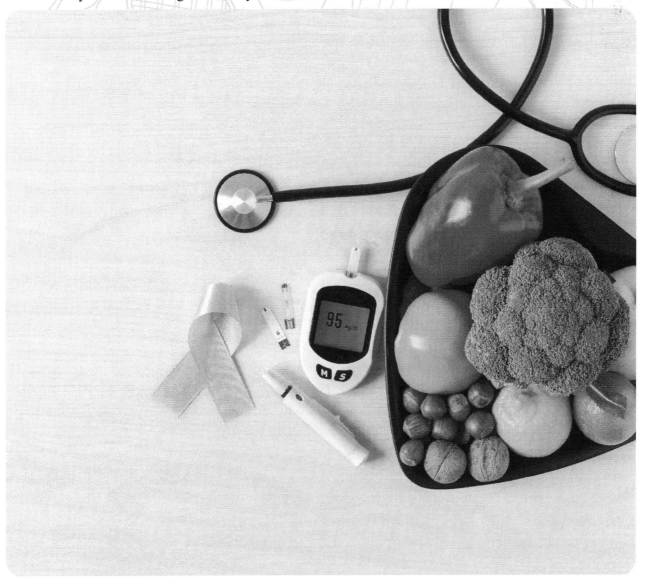

# A Short Story About Smith

Smith, a devoted worker in the bright center of New York City, faced a chronic challenge: regulating her blood glucose levels. Despite her best attempts, she became entangled in the erratic rhythms of shifting health.

Smith confided in her close friend Maya, who was frustrated and felt lost in a sea of contradicting nutritional recommendations. Maya, sensing Smith's distress, told stories about the legendary "Glucose Goddess Cookbook." This mythical book was said to contain culinary marvels capable of balancing blood sugar levels while satisfying the senses.

Smith set off on a mission to find this elusive cookbook, propelled by hope and resolve. She finally found a copy in a secluded nook of a downtown bookshop after scouring bookstores and libraries for hours.

Smith scanned over the cookbook's pages, each one a monument to culinary skill, anxious to discover its secrets. The menus were a blend of healthful ingredients and unique flavors, painstakingly tailored for blood glucose management, and ranged from vivid salads to hefty mains and seductive desserts.

Smith entered her kitchen with increased zest, armed with newfound inspiration. She followed the cookbook's advice, saying goodbye to processed sweets and refined carbohydrates in favor of healthy whole grains, fresh veggies, and lean meats.

Smith engaged herself in the culinary adventures inspired by the "Glucose Goddess Cookbook" with each passing day. She discovered the thrill of preparing meals that not only satisfied her palate but also nourished her body by keeping her blood glucose levels stable.

Her kitchen evolved into a laboratory for exploration, where the art of harmonizing tastes and nutrition melded flawlessly. Smith's experience with the cookbook became a tribute to her strength and newfound control over her health.

Smith discovered a road to not just regulating her blood glucose but also tasting life's tastes with increased appreciation thanks to the knowledge of the "Glucose Goddess Cookbook." Her path proved the transformational power of education, dedication, and the culinary magic contained inside those treasured pages.

# Foods to Avoid and Food to Eat to Control Blood Glucose

| Foods to Avoid | Foods to Eat |
|---|---|
| Sugary beverages (sodas, fruit juices) | Leafy green vegetables |
| Processed sweets (candy, pastries) | Whole grains (brown rice, quinoa) |
| High-sugar cereals | Lean protein sources (chicken, fish, tofu) |
| White bread and refined grains | Healthy fats (avocado, nuts, seeds) |
| Fried foods | Fresh fruits in moderation (berries, apples) |
| High-fat dairy products | Legumes (beans, lentils) |
| Excessive red meat | Low-fat dairy (skim milk, yogurt) |
| Packaged snacks with added sugars | Foods high in fiber (oats, barley) |
|  |  |
|  |  |
|  |  |
|  |  |
|  |  |
|  |  |

# 30-DAY MEAL PLAN

| DAY | BREAK FAST SMOOTHIE | LUNCH | DINNER |
|:---:|---|---|---|
| 1 | Berry Blast Smoothie | Grilled Chicken Salad | Spinach and Pineapple Smoothie |
| 2 | Green Power Smoothie | Quinoa Salad | Blueberry Almond Smoothie |
| 3 | Tropical Paradise Smoothie | Veggie Wrap | Raspberry Coconut Smoothie |
| 4 | Chocolate Banana Protein Smoothie | Lentil Soup | Apple Cinnamon Smoothie |
| 5 | Mango Ginger Smoothie | Tuna Salad Sandwich | Strawberry Spinach Smoothie |
| 6 | Blueberry Almond Smoothie | Veggie Stir-Fry | Orange Carrot Ginger Smoothie |
| 7 | Kale and Kiwi Smoothie | Baked Sweet Potatoes | Mixed Berry Greek Yogurt Smoothie |
| 8 | Avocado Banana Smoothie | Chickpea Salad | Pomegranate Berry Smoothie |
| 9 | Papaya Lime Smoothie | Tomato Basil Pasta | Peach and Oat Smoothie |
| 10 | Watermelon Mint Smoothie | Veggie Burger | Cherry Almond Butter Smoothie |
| 11 | Spinach and Mango Smoothie | Quinoa Bowl | Cranberry Walnut Smoothie |
| 12 | Pineapple Turmeric Smoothie | Black Bean Soup | Fig and Honey Smoothie |
| 13 | Cantaloupe Basil Smoothie | Veggie Stir-Fry | Cantaloupe Basil Smoothie |
| 14 | Blackberry Chia Seed Smoothie | Mediterranean Salad | Pumpkin Pie Smoothie |
| 15 | Blueberry Avocado Smoothie | Veggie Wrap | Lentil and Spinach Soup |

# 30-DAY MEAL PLAN

| DAY | BREAK FAST SMOOTHIES | LUNCH | DINNER |
|-----|---------------------|-------|--------|
| 16 | Honeydew Mint Smoothie | Lentil Curry | Honeydew Mint Smoothie |
| 17 | Mixed Berries Greek Yogurt Smoothie | Quinoa Salad | Mixed Berries Greek Yogurt Smoothie |
| 18 | Beetroot and Berry Smoothie | Chickpea Bowl | Cherry Cocoa Smoothie |
| 19 | Apricot Almond Smoothie | Stuffed Bell Peppers | Lemon Raspberry Smoothie |
| 20 | Carrot Cake Smoothie | Veggie Stir-Fry | Mango Coconut Chia Smoothie |
| 21 | Mango Coconut Chia Smoothie | Greek Salad | Green Tea Berry Smoothie |
| 22 | Banana Walnut Protein Smoothie | Tomato Soup | Raspberry Pistachio Smoothie |
| 23 | Pineapple Turmeric Ginger Smoothie | Veggie Wrap | Papaya Coconut Smoothie |
| 24 | Cucumber Melon Smoothie | Lentil Salad | Orange Creamsicle Smoothie |
| 25 | Date and Almond Smoothie | Mediterranean Bowl | Strawberry Basil Smoothie |
| 26 | Blueberry Flaxseed Smoothie | Quinoa Stir-Fry | Berry Blast Smoothie |
| 27 | Apple Kale Spinach Smoothie | Veggie Sandwich | Green Power Smoothie |
| 28 | Dragon Fruit Pineapple Smoothie | Baked Potato Soup | Tropical Paradise Smoothie |
| 29 | Raspberry Mint Smoothie | Greek Wrap | Chocolate Banana Protein Smoothie |
| 30 | Papaya Coconut Smoothie | Cauliflower Curry | Mango Ginger Smoothie |

# Recipes

# BREAKFAST RECIPES

## QUINOA SALAD WITH ROASTED VEGETABLES

### INGREDIENTS

- 1 cup quinoa
- 2 cups vegetable broth or water
- 2 cups assorted vegetables (bell peppers, zucchini, cherry tomatoes, red onion)
- 2 tablespoons olive oil
- Salt and pepper to taste
- 1/4 cup chopped fresh herbs (parsley, basil)
- Juice of 1 lemon
- Optional: Feta cheese for garnish

### PREPARATION

1. Preheat oven to 400°F (200°C).
2. Rinse quinoa under cold water and cook it in vegetable broth according to package instructions.
3. Chop the assorted vegetables into bite-sized pieces and toss them with olive oil, salt, and pepper.
4. Spread the vegetables on a baking sheet and roast for 20-25 minutes until they're tender and slightly charred.
5. In a large bowl, combine cooked quinoa, roasted vegetables, chopped herbs, lemon juice, and toss to mix.
6. Taste and adjust seasoning if needed. Garnish with crumbled feta cheese if desired. Serve warm or at room temperature.

## LEMON HERB BAKED CHICKEN

### INGREDIENTS

- 4 boneless, skinless chicken breasts
- 2 tablespoons olive oil
- 2 cloves garlic, minced
- Zest and juice of 1 lemon
- 1 teaspoon dried thyme
- 1 teaspoon dried rosemary
- Salt and pepper to taste

### PREPARATION

1. Preheat oven to 375°F (190°C).
2. Place chicken breasts in a baking dish.
3. In a small bowl, mix olive oil, minced garlic, lemon zest, lemon juice, dried thyme, dried rosemary, salt, and pepper.
4. Pour the herb mixture over the chicken, ensuring it's evenly coated.
5. Bake for 25-30 minutes or until the chicken reaches an internal temperature of 165°F (74°C).
6. Remove from oven, let it rest for a few minutes, then serve.

## BLACK BEAN AND SWEET POTATO TACOS

### INGREDIENTS

- 1 tablespoon olive oil
- 1 sweet potato, peeled and diced
- 1 can (15 oz) black beans, drained and rinsed
- 1 teaspoon chili powder
- 1/2 teaspoon cumin
- Salt and pepper to taste
- Corn or flour tortillas
- Toppings: Avocado slices, diced tomatoes, shredded lettuce, salsa, Greek yogurt (optional)

### PREPARATION

1. Heat olive oil in a skillet over medium heat. Add diced sweet potato and sauté until tender, about 8-10 minutes.
2. Add black beans, chili powder, cumin, salt, and pepper to the skillet. Cook for an additional 2-3 minutes until heated through.
3. Warm tortillas in a separate skillet or microwave.
4. Spoon the sweet potato and black bean mixture into tortillas.
5. Top with desired toppings like avocado slices, diced tomatoes, shredded lettuce, salsa, or Greek yogurt.

## GARLIC AND HERB ROASTED SALMON

### INGREDIENTS

- 4 salmon fillets
- 2 cloves garlic, minced
- 2 tablespoons olive oil
- 1 tablespoon chopped fresh parsley
- 1 tablespoon chopped fresh dill (or 1 teaspoon dried dill)
- Salt and pepper to taste
- Lemon wedges for serving

### PREPARATION

1. Preheat oven to 400°F (200°C).
2. Place salmon fillets on a baking sheet lined with parchment paper or foil.
3. In a small bowl, mix minced garlic, olive oil, chopped parsley, chopped dill, salt, and pepper.
4. Brush the herb mixture over the salmon fillets, covering them evenly.
5. Roast in the oven for 12-15 minutes until the salmon is cooked through and flakes easily with a fork.
6. Serve with lemon wedges on the side.

# CAULIFLOWER FRIED RICE

## INGREDIENTS

- 1 head cauliflower, grated or processed into rice-like texture
- 2 tablespoons sesame oil
- 2 cloves garlic, minced
- 1 cup mixed vegetables (peas, carrots, bell peppers)
- 2 eggs, beaten (optional)
- 3 tablespoons low-sodium soy sauce or tamari
- Salt and pepper to taste
- Green onions for garnish (optional)

## PREPARATION

1. Heat sesame oil in a large skillet or wok over medium heat. Add minced garlic and sauté for 30 seconds.
2. Add the mixed vegetables and stir-fry for 3-4 minutes until they begin to soften.
3. Push the vegetables to one side of the skillet and pour the beaten eggs into the other side (if using). Scramble the eggs until cooked.
4. Add the cauliflower rice to the skillet and stir-fry for 4-5 minutes until it's heated through.
5. Pour soy sauce or tamari over the cauliflower rice, and mix well. Season with salt and pepper.
6. Garnish with chopped green onions if desired and serve hot.

# GRILLED VEGETABLE SKEWERS WITH TOFU

## INGREDIENTS

- 1 block firm tofu, pressed and cubed
- Assorted vegetables (bell peppers, zucchini, cherry tomatoes, red onion)
- 2 tablespoons olive oil
- 2 cloves garlic, minced
- 1 teaspoon dried herbs (oregano, thyme, rosemary)
- Salt and pepper to taste
- Wooden skewers, soaked in water

## PREPARATION

1. Preheat the grill to medium-high heat.
2. Thread the cubed tofu and assorted vegetables onto the soaked skewers.
3. In a small bowl, mix olive oil, minced garlic, dried herbs, salt, and pepper.
4. Brush the olive oil mixture over the skewered tofu and vegetables.
5. Place the skewers on the grill and cook for 10-12 minutes, turning occasionally until the vegetables are charred and the tofu is lightly browned.
6. Serve the grilled vegetable skewers hot.

# MEDITERRANEAN CHICKPEA SALAD

## INGREDIENTS

- 2 cans (15 oz each) chickpeas, drained and rinsed
- 1 cucumber, diced
- 1 cup cherry tomatoes, halved
- 1/2 red onion, thinly sliced
- 1/4 cup chopped fresh parsley
- 1/4 cup chopped fresh mint
- 3 tablespoons olive oil
- Juice of 1 lemon
- 2 teaspoons red wine vinegar
- Salt and pepper to taste
- Feta cheese (optional)

## PREPARATION

1. In a large mixing bowl, combine chickpeas, diced cucumber, halved cherry tomatoes, sliced red onion, chopped parsley, and chopped mint.
2. In a separate small bowl, whisk together olive oil, lemon juice, red wine vinegar, salt, and pepper to make the dressing.
3. Pour the dressing over the salad ingredients and toss gently to coat everything evenly.
4. Crumble feta cheese over the salad if desired.
5. Refrigerate for at least 30 minutes before serving to allow flavors to meld.

# TURKEY AND VEGGIE STUFFED PEPPERS

## INGREDIENTS

- 4 bell peppers, tops removed and seeds removed
- 1 pound ground turkey
- 1 cup cooked brown rice
- 1 cup diced tomatoes
- 1 cup chopped spinach
- 1/2 cup grated mozzarella cheese
- 2 cloves garlic, minced
- 1 teaspoon dried Italian seasoning
- Salt and pepper to taste

## PREPARATION

1. Preheat oven to 375°F (190°C).
2. In a skillet, cook ground turkey over medium heat until no longer pink. Drain excess fat if needed.
3. Add minced garlic and chopped spinach to the skillet and sauté for a few minutes until the spinach wilts.
4. Stir in cooked brown rice, diced tomatoes, dried Italian seasoning, salt, and pepper. Cook for an additional 2-3 minutes.
5. Spoon the turkey and veggie mixture into the hollowed-out bell peppers.
6. Place the stuffed peppers in a baking dish and cover with foil. Bake for 25-30 minutes.
7. Remove the foil, sprinkle grated mozzarella cheese on top of each pepper, and bake uncovered for an additional 5-7 minutes until the cheese melts and peppers are tender.

# SPINACH AND FETA STUFFED CHICKEN BREAST

## INGREDIENTS

- 4 boneless, skinless chicken breasts
- 2 cups fresh spinach leaves
- 1/2 cup crumbled feta cheese
- 2 cloves garlic, minced
- 1 tablespoon olive oil
- Salt and pepper to taste

## PREPARATION

1. Preheat oven to 375°F (190°C).
2. Using a sharp knife, create a pocket in each chicken breast without cutting all the way through.
3. In a skillet, heat olive oil over medium heat. Add minced garlic and sauté for 30 seconds.
4. Add fresh spinach to the skillet and cook until wilted.
5. Remove the skillet from heat and let the spinach cool slightly. Stir in crumbled feta cheese.
6. Stuff each chicken breast with the spinach and feta mixture. Secure with toothpicks if needed.
7. Place the stuffed chicken breasts in a baking dish. Season the outside with salt and pepper.
8. Bake for 25-30 minutes or until the chicken is cooked through and reaches an internal temperature of 165°F (74°C).
9. Allow the chicken to rest for a few minutes before serving.

# ZUCCHINI NOODLES WITH PESTO

## INGREDIENTS

- 4 medium-sized zucchinis
- 1 cup fresh basil leaves
- 1/4 cup pine nuts or walnuts
- 2 cloves garlic, minced
- 1/4 cup grated Parmesan cheese (optional)
- 1/3 cup olive oil
- Salt and pepper to taste

## PREPARATION

1. Using a spiralizer or vegetable peeler, create zucchini noodles (zoodles) from the zucchinis.
2. In a food processor, combine basil leaves, pine nuts or walnuts, minced garlic, and Parmesan cheese (if using). Pulse until finely chopped.
3. With the food processor running, slowly drizzle in the olive oil until the pesto reaches your desired consistency. Season with salt and pepper.
4. In a large skillet, heat a small amount of olive oil over medium heat. Add zucchini noodles and sauté for 2-3 minutes until they're slightly softened.
5. Toss the zucchini noodles with the prepared pesto until they're evenly coated.
6. Serve the zucchini noodles with additional grated Parmesan cheese on top if desired.

# LENTIL SOUP WITH KALE

## INGREDIENTS

- 1 cup dried lentils, rinsed
- 1 onion, diced
- 2 carrots, diced
- 2 celery stalks, diced
- 3 cloves garlic, minced
- 6 cups vegetable broth
- 2 cups chopped kale
- 1 teaspoon dried thyme
- Salt and pepper to taste
- Olive oil for cooking

## PREPARATION

1. Heat olive oil in a large pot over medium heat. Add onions, carrots, celery, and garlic. Sauté until onions are translucent.
2. Add lentils, vegetable broth, thyme, salt, and pepper. Bring to a boil, then reduce heat to simmer. Cover and cook for about 20-25 minutes or until lentils are tender.
3. Stir in chopped kale and simmer for an additional 5-10 minutes until kale is wilted. Adjust seasoning if needed. Serve hot.

# BAKED COD WITH TOMATO SALSA

## INGREDIENTS

- 4 cod fillets
- 2 cups diced tomatoes
- 1/4 cup chopped fresh cilantro
- 1/2 red onion, finely chopped
- 2 tablespoons lime juice
- 2 cloves garlic, minced
- Salt and pepper to taste
- Olive oil

## PREPARATION

1. Preheat oven to 375°F (190°C).
2. Season cod fillets with salt and pepper. Place them on a baking dish lined with parchment paper.
3. In a bowl, mix diced tomatoes, cilantro, red onion, lime juice, garlic, salt, and pepper to make the salsa.
4. Spoon the tomato salsa over the cod fillets.
5. Drizzle a little olive oil over the top. Bake for 15-20 minutes or until the fish flakes easily with a fork. Serve hot.

# RATATOUILLE WITH HERBED QUINOA

## INGREDIENTS

- 1 eggplant, diced
- 1 zucchini, diced
- 1 yellow squash, diced
- 1 red bell pepper, diced
- 1 onion, chopped
- 3 cloves garlic, minced
- 2 cups diced tomatoes
- 2 teaspoons dried Italian herbs
- 1 cup quinoa
- 2 cups vegetable broth
- Olive oil
- Salt and pepper to taste

## PREPARATION

1. Heat olive oil in a large skillet over medium heat. Add onion and garlic, sauté until softened.
2. Add eggplant, zucchini, yellow squash, and bell pepper. Cook for about 8-10 minutes until vegetables are tender.
3. Stir in diced tomatoes, Italian herbs, salt, and pepper. Simmer for 10-15 minutes.
4. Meanwhile, rinse quinoa and cook it in vegetable broth according to package instructions.
5. Serve ratatouille over cooked herbed quinoa.

# TERIYAKI TOFU STIR-FRY

## INGREDIENTS

- 14 oz (400g) extra-firm tofu, drained and cubed
- 2 tablespoons soy sauce
- 2 tablespoons rice vinegar
- 1 tablespoon honey or maple syrup
- 2 cloves garlic, minced
- 1 teaspoon grated ginger
- 1 tablespoon sesame oil
- 2 cups mixed vegetables (bell peppers, broccoli, carrots)
- Cooked brown rice for serving
- Sesame seeds and chopped green onions for garnish

## PREPARATION

1. In a bowl, mix soy sauce, rice vinegar, honey or maple syrup, garlic, and ginger. Marinate the tofu cubes in this mixture for about 15-20 minutes.
2. Heat sesame oil in a skillet over medium-high heat. Add marinated tofu and stir-fry until golden brown. Remove tofu from the pan and set aside.
3. In the same pan, stir-fry mixed vegetables until tender-crisp.
4. Return the tofu to the pan, add any remaining marinade, and toss everything together for a minute.
5. Serve the teriyaki tofu stir-fry over cooked brown rice. Garnish with sesame seeds and chopped green onions.

## GREEK YOGURT AND BERRY PARFAIT

### INGREDIENTS

- 1 cup Greek yogurt
- 1 cup mixed berries (strawberries, blueberries, raspberries)
- 1 tablespoon honey or agave syrup (optional)
- Granola or chopped nuts for topping (optional)

### PREPARATION

1. In a bowl, mix Greek yogurt with honey or agave syrup if desired.
2. In serving glasses or bowls, layer the Greek yogurt alternately with mixed berries.
3. Repeat layers until glasses are filled.
4. Top with granola or chopped nuts for added crunch if desired. Serve chilled.

## EGGPLANT LASAGNA WITH RICOTTA AND SPINACH

### INGREDIENTS

- 2 large eggplants, thinly sliced lengthwise
- 2 cups ricotta cheese
- 1 cup chopped spinach
- 2 cups marinara sauce
- 1 cup shredded mozzarella cheese
- 1/2 cup grated Parmesan cheese
- Italian seasoning, salt, and pepper to taste
- Olive oil

### PREPARATION

1. Preheat oven to 375°F (190°C). Brush eggplant slices with olive oil and roast in the oven for 15-20 minutes until tender. Remove and set aside.
2. In a bowl, mix ricotta cheese, chopped spinach, Italian seasoning, salt, and pepper.
3. In a baking dish, spread a layer of marinara sauce. Place a layer of roasted eggplant slices over the sauce.
4. Spread the ricotta-spinach mixture over the eggplant. Repeat layers, finishing with marinara sauce on top.
5. Sprinkle mozzarella and Parmesan cheese on top. Cover with foil and bake for 30 minutes. Uncover and bake for an additional 10 minutes until cheese is bubbly and golden.

# TURKEY MEATBALLS IN MARINARA SAUCE

## INGREDIENTS

- 1 lb (450g) ground turkey
- 1/2 cup breadcrumbs (preferably whole wheat)
- 1/4 cup grated Parmesan cheese
- 1 egg
- 2 cloves garlic, minced
- 1 teaspoon Italian seasoning
- Salt and pepper to taste
- 2 cups marinara sauce
- Olive oil

## PREPARATION

1. Preheat oven to 375°F (190°C).
2. In a bowl, mix ground turkey, breadcrumbs, Parmesan cheese, egg, minced garlic, Italian seasoning, salt, and pepper.
3. Shape the mixture into meatballs and place them on a baking sheet lined with parchment paper.
4. Bake meatballs in the preheated oven for 20-25 minutes or until cooked through.
5. Heat marinara sauce in a saucepan. Add the baked meatballs and simmer for a few minutes until heated through. Serve hot.

# STUFFED PORTOBELLO MUSHROOMS

## INGREDIENTS

- 4 large portobello mushrooms
- 1 cup quinoa, cooked
- 1 cup chopped spinach
- 1/2 cup diced tomatoes
- 1/4 cup grated Parmesan cheese
- 2 cloves garlic, minced
- 1 tablespoon olive oil
- Salt and pepper to taste
- Fresh parsley for garnish

## PREPARATION

1. Preheat oven to 375°F (190°C). Remove the stems from the portobello mushrooms and gently clean the caps.
2. In a skillet, heat olive oil over medium heat. Sauté minced garlic until fragrant.
3. Add chopped spinach and cook until wilted. Stir in cooked quinoa, diced tomatoes, Parmesan cheese, salt, and pepper. Cook for a few minutes until combined.
4. Stuff the portobello mushroom caps with the quinoa-spinach mixture.
5. Place the stuffed mushrooms on a baking sheet and bake for 20-25 minutes until mushrooms are tender and filling is heated through.
6. Garnish with fresh parsley before serving.

# CABBAGE AND BEEF STIR-FRY

## INGREDIENTS

- 1 lb (450g) lean ground beef
- 4 cups shredded cabbage
- 1 red bell pepper, sliced
- 1 onion, thinly sliced
- 3 cloves garlic, minced
- 2 tablespoons low-sodium soy sauce
- 1 tablespoon rice vinegar
- 1 teaspoon sesame oil
- 1 teaspoon grated ginger
- Salt and pepper to taste
- Olive oil

## PREPARATION

1. Heat olive oil in a large skillet or wok over medium-high heat. Add minced garlic and grated ginger, sauté until fragrant.
2. Add ground beef and cook until browned, breaking it apart with a spoon.
3. Stir in sliced bell pepper and onion. Cook for a few minutes until vegetables are slightly tender.
4. Add shredded cabbage, soy sauce, rice vinegar, sesame oil, salt, and pepper. Stir-fry for an additional 3-4 minutes until cabbage is wilted but still crisp. Adjust seasoning if needed. Serve hot.

# BROCCOLI AND CHEDDAR QUICHE WITH ALMOND FLOUR CRUST

## INGREDIENTS

### For the Almond Flour Crust

- 1 1/2 cups almond flour
- 1/4 cup melted coconut oil or butter
- 1 egg
- 1/2 teaspoon salt

### For the Quiche Filling

- 2 cups broccoli florets, blanched and chopped
- 1 cup shredded cheddar cheese
- 4 eggs
- 1 cup milk or almond milk
- Salt and pepper to taste

## PREPARATION

### For the Almond Flour Crust

1. Preheat oven to 350°F (175°C).
2. In a bowl, mix almond flour, melted coconut oil or butter, egg, and salt until well combined.
3. Press the mixture into a pie dish to form the crust. Bake for 10-12 minutes until lightly golden. Remove from oven and set aside.

### For the Quiche Filling

1. Spread blanched and chopped broccoli florets evenly over the pre-baked crust. Sprinkle shredded cheddar cheese on top.
2. In another bowl, whisk together eggs, milk, salt, and pepper. Pour the egg mixture over the broccoli and cheese.
3. Bake the quiche in the preheated oven for 30-35 minutes or until the center is set and the top is golden brown. Remove from oven and let it cool slightly before slicing and serving.

# SPICY SHRIMP LETTUCE WRAPS

## INGREDIENTS

- 1 pound large shrimp, peeled and deveined
- 2 tablespoons olive oil
- 2 cloves garlic, minced
- 1 teaspoon ginger, minced
- 2 tablespoons soy sauce
- 1 tablespoon sriracha sauce
- 1 tablespoon honey
- 1 tablespoon lime juice
- Salt and pepper to taste
- Butter lettuce leaves
- Optional toppings: chopped peanuts, cilantro, sliced green onions

## PREPARATION

1. In a bowl, mix together soy sauce, sriracha, honey, and lime juice to create the sauce.
2. Heat olive oil in a skillet over medium heat. Add minced garlic and ginger, sauté for a minute.
3. Add shrimp to the skillet and cook until they turn pink, about 2-3 minutes.
4. Pour the prepared sauce over the shrimp, stirring well to coat. Cook for an additional minute until the sauce thickens slightly.
5. Season with salt and pepper to taste.
6. Spoon the spicy shrimp mixture into butter lettuce leaves. Garnish with chopped peanuts, cilantro, and sliced green onions if desired.

# OVEN-BAKED GARLIC PARMESAN CAULIFLOWER BITES

## INGREDIENTS

- 1 head cauliflower, cut into florets
- 1/2 cup grated Parmesan cheese
- 1 teaspoon garlic powder
- 1/2 teaspoon paprika
- Salt and pepper to taste
- 2 tablespoons olive oil
- Chopped fresh parsley (optional for garnish)

## PREPARATION

1. Preheat the oven to 400°F (200°C) and line a baking sheet with parchment paper.
2. In a large bowl, toss cauliflower florets with olive oil, garlic powder, paprika, salt, and pepper until coated evenly.
3. Spread the seasoned cauliflower florets onto the prepared baking sheet in a single layer.
4. Bake in the preheated oven for 20-25 minutes or until the cauliflower is tender and golden brown.
5. Sprinkle grated Parmesan cheese over the cauliflower and bake for an additional 5 minutes until the cheese is melted and slightly crispy.
6. Garnish with chopped fresh parsley before serving.

# CHICKEN AND BROCCOLI SKILLET

## INGREDIENTS

- 1 pound boneless, skinless chicken breasts, cut into cubes
- 2 tablespoons olive oil
- 3 cups broccoli florets
- 2 cloves garlic, minced
- 1 teaspoon paprika
- 1/2 teaspoon red pepper flakes (adjust to taste)
- Salt and pepper to taste
- 1/4 cup low-sodium chicken broth
- Juice of 1 lemon
- Chopped fresh parsley for garnish

## PREPARATION

1. Heat olive oil in a large skillet over medium-high heat.
2. Add the cubed chicken to the skillet and cook until browned and cooked through. Remove the chicken from the skillet and set aside.
3. In the same skillet, add garlic and broccoli florets. Sauté for a few minutes until the broccoli is tender-crisp.
4. Return the cooked chicken to the skillet. Sprinkle paprika, red pepper flakes, salt, and pepper over the mixture, stirring to combine.
5. Pour in the chicken broth and lemon juice, stirring well. Let it simmer for a few minutes until the sauce slightly thickens.
6. Garnish with chopped parsley before serving.

# AVOCADO AND CHICKPEA SALAD

## INGREDIENTS

- 2 ripe avocados, diced
- 1 can (15 oz) chickpeas, drained and rinsed
- 1 cup cherry tomatoes, halved
- 1/4 cup red onion, finely chopped
- 2 tablespoons fresh cilantro or parsley, chopped
- Juice of 1 lime
- 2 tablespoons olive oil
- Salt and pepper to taste

## PREPARATION

1. In a large bowl, combine diced avocado, chickpeas, cherry tomatoes, red onion, and chopped cilantro or parsley.
2. Drizzle olive oil and lime juice over the salad. Gently toss to coat all ingredients.
3. Season with salt and pepper according to taste.
4. Serve chilled.

# BAKED HALIBUT WITH HERBS

## INGREDIENTS

- 4 halibut fillets (about 6 oz each)
- 2 tablespoons olive oil
- 2 cloves garlic, minced
- 1 tablespoon fresh parsley, chopped
- 1 tablespoon fresh dill, chopped
- 1 tablespoon fresh chives, chopped
- Salt and pepper to taste
- Lemon wedges for serving

## PREPARATION

1. Preheat the oven to 400°F (200°C) and grease a baking dish.
2. Place halibut fillets in the prepared baking dish.
3. In a small bowl, mix together olive oil, minced garlic, chopped parsley, dill, chives, salt, and pepper.
4. Brush the herb mixture evenly over each halibut fillet.
5. Bake in the preheated oven for 12-15 minutes or until the fish is cooked through and flakes easily with a fork.
6. Serve with lemon wedges.

# QUINOA-STUFFED BELL PEPPERS

## INGREDIENTS

- 4 large bell peppers, tops removed and seeds removed
- 1 cup quinoa, cooked
- 1 can (15 oz) black beans, drained and rinsed
- 1 cup corn kernels (fresh, frozen, or canned)
- 1 cup diced tomatoes
- 1 teaspoon cumin
- 1/2 teaspoon chili powder
- 1/2 teaspoon paprika
- Salt and pepper to taste
- Shredded cheese for topping (optional)
- Chopped fresh cilantro for garnish

## PREPARATION

1. Preheat the oven to 375°F (190°C) and grease a baking dish.
2. In a mixing bowl, combine cooked quinoa, black beans, corn, diced tomatoes, cumin, chili powder, paprika, salt, and pepper.
3. Stuff each bell pepper with the quinoa mixture and place them in the prepared baking dish.
4. If desired, sprinkle shredded cheese on top of each stuffed pepper.
5. Cover the baking dish with foil and bake for 25-30 minutes or until the peppers are tender.
6. Garnish with chopped cilantro before serving.

# THAI-INSPIRED VEGGIE NOODLE SOUP

## INGREDIENTS

- 6 cups vegetable or chicken broth
- 8 oz rice noodles or spiralized vegetables
- 1 cup sliced shiitake mushrooms
- 1 cup broccoli florets
- 1 red bell pepper, thinly sliced
- 1 carrot, julienned
- 1 can (14 oz) coconut milk
- 2 tablespoons soy sauce
- 2 tablespoons fresh lime juice
- 2 teaspoons fresh ginger, grated
- 2 cloves garlic, minced
- Fresh cilantro and sliced green onions for garnish

## PREPARATION

1. In a large pot, bring the broth to a boil. Add rice noodles or spiralized vegetables and cook according to package instructions.
2. Reduce heat to medium-low and add sliced shiitake mushrooms, broccoli florets, red bell pepper, and julienned carrot to the pot.
3. In a separate bowl, mix coconut milk, soy sauce, lime juice, grated ginger, and minced garlic. Add this mixture to the pot, stirring well.
4. Simmer the soup for a few minutes until the vegetables are tender.
5. Serve hot, garnished with fresh cilantro and sliced green onions.

# CAULIFLOWER AND CHICKPEA CURRY

## INGREDIENTS

- 1 head cauliflower, cut into florets
- 1 can (15 oz) chickpeas, drained and rinsed
- 1 onion, finely chopped
- 3 cloves garlic, minced
- 1 tablespoon ginger, grated
- 2 tablespoons curry powder
- 1 teaspoon ground turmeric
- 1 can (14 oz) diced tomatoes
- 1 can (14 oz) coconut milk
- 2 tablespoons olive oil
- Salt and pepper to taste
- Fresh cilantro for garnish

## PREPARATION

1. Heat olive oil in a large skillet or pot over medium heat. Add chopped onion, minced garlic, and grated ginger. Sauté until fragrant.
2. Add cauliflower florets and chickpeas to the skillet, stirring for a few minutes.
3. Sprinkle curry powder and turmeric over the mixture, stirring to coat evenly.
4. Pour in diced tomatoes and coconut milk, stirring well. Bring to a gentle simmer.
5. Cover and cook for about 15-20 minutes or until the cauliflower is tender.
6. Season with salt and pepper according to taste.
7. Garnish with fresh cilantro before serving.

# TURKEY AND VEGETABLE SKILLET

## INGREDIENTS

- 1 pound ground turkey
- 1 tablespoon olive oil
- 1 onion, diced
- 2 cloves garlic, minced
- 1 red bell pepper, diced
- 1 zucchini, diced
- 1 cup cherry tomatoes, halved
- 1 teaspoon dried oregano
- 1 teaspoon paprika
- Salt and pepper to taste
- Fresh parsley for garnish

## PREPARATION

1. Heat olive oil in a large skillet over medium-high heat.
2. Add diced onion and minced garlic to the skillet, sauté until softened.
3. Add ground turkey to the skillet, breaking it apart with a spoon, and cook until browned.
4. Stir in diced red bell pepper, zucchini, and cherry tomatoes. Cook for a few minutes until vegetables are tender.
5. Sprinkle dried oregano, paprika, salt, and pepper over the mixture, stirring well.
6. Cook for an additional 5 minutes until flavors meld together.
7. Garnish with fresh parsley before serving.

# CAPRESE SALAD WITH BALSAMIC GLAZE

## INGREDIENTS

- 4 large ripe tomatoes, sliced
- 1 pound fresh mozzarella cheese, sliced
- Fresh basil leaves
- Balsamic glaze (store-bought or homemade)
- Extra virgin olive oil
- Salt and pepper to taste

## PREPARATION

1. Arrange sliced tomatoes and fresh mozzarella alternately on a serving platter.
2. Tuck fresh basil leaves between the tomato and mozzarella slices.
3. Drizzle extra virgin olive oil over the salad.
4. Season with salt and pepper according to taste.
5. Drizzle balsamic glaze generously over the salad just before serving.

# BAKED SWEET POTATO FRIES

## INGREDIENTS

- 2 large sweet potatoes, washed and cut into fries
- 2 tablespoons olive oil
- 1 teaspoon paprika
- 1/2 teaspoon garlic powder
- Salt and pepper to taste

## PREPARATION

1. Preheat the oven to 425°F (220°C) and line a baking sheet with parchment paper.
2. In a large bowl, toss the sweet potato fries with olive oil, paprika, garlic powder, salt, and pepper until evenly coated.
3. Spread the fries on the prepared baking sheet in a single layer.
4. Bake for 20-25 minutes, flipping halfway through, until the fries are crispy and golden brown.

# LEMON GARLIC SHRIMP SKEWERS

## INGREDIENTS

- 1 pound large shrimp, peeled and deveined
- 3 cloves garlic, minced
- Zest and juice of 1 lemon
- 2 tablespoons olive oil
- 1 teaspoon dried oregano
- Salt and pepper to taste
- Wooden skewers, soaked in water

## PREPARATION

1. In a bowl, combine minced garlic, lemon zest, lemon juice, olive oil, oregano, salt, and pepper.
2. Add the shrimp to the marinade, toss to coat, and let it marinate for 20-30 minutes in the refrigerator.
3. Preheat grill or grill pan over medium-high heat.
4. Thread the marinated shrimp onto the soaked skewers.
5. Grill the shrimp skewers for 2-3 minutes per side or until they turn pink and opaque.

# SPINACH AND MUSHROOM QUICHE CUPS

## INGREDIENTS

- 6 large eggs
- 1/2 cup milk (or milk alternative)
- 1 cup chopped spinach
- 1 cup sliced mushrooms
- 1/2 cup shredded cheese (such as cheddar or Swiss)
- Salt and pepper to taste

## PREPARATION

1. Preheat the oven to 375°F (190°C) and grease a muffin tin.
2. In a bowl, whisk together eggs, milk, salt, and pepper.
3. Divide chopped spinach, sliced mushrooms, and shredded cheese evenly among the muffin cups.
4. Pour the egg mixture over the vegetables and cheese, filling each cup almost to the top.
5. Bake for 20-25 minutes or until the quiche cups are set and lightly golden on top.

# TOMATO BASIL CHICKEN WITH ZOODLES

## INGREDIENTS

- 4 boneless, skinless chicken breasts
- 2 tablespoons olive oil
- 2 cloves garlic, minced
- 1 can (14 oz) diced tomatoes
- 1/4 cup fresh basil leaves, chopped
- Salt and pepper to taste
- Zucchini, spiralized into "zoodles"

## PREPARATION

1. Season the chicken breasts with salt and pepper.
2. In a skillet, heat olive oil over medium heat. Add minced garlic and sauté until fragrant.
3. Add the chicken breasts to the skillet and cook until golden brown on each side and cooked through, about 6-8 minutes per side. Remove and set aside.
4. In the same skillet, add diced tomatoes (with their juices) and chopped basil. Stir and simmer for a few minutes.
5. Add the zucchini "zoodles" to the skillet and toss until heated through and coated in the tomato basil sauce.
6. Serve the cooked chicken over the zoodles with the tomato basil sauce.

# VEGGIE-PACKED MINESTRONE SOUP

## INGREDIENTS

- 1 tablespoon olive oil
- 1 onion, chopped
- 2 cloves garlic, minced
- 2 carrots, diced
- 2 celery stalks, diced
- 1 can (14 oz) diced tomatoes
- 6 cups vegetable broth
- 1 can (15 oz) kidney beans, drained and rinsed
- 1 cup small pasta (such as ditalini)
- 2 cups chopped spinach
- Salt and pepper to taste
- Fresh basil leaves for garnish (optional)

## PREPARATION

1. In a large pot, heat olive oil over medium heat. Add chopped onion and sauté until translucent.
2. Add minced garlic, diced carrots, and diced celery. Sauté for a few minutes until vegetables soften.
3. Pour in diced tomatoes, vegetable broth, and drained kidney beans. Bring to a simmer.
4. Add the pasta to the pot and cook according to package instructions.
5. Stir in chopped spinach and cook until wilted. Season with salt and pepper.
6. Serve hot, garnished with fresh basil leaves if desired.

# CAULIFLOWER PIZZA CRUST WITH ASSORTED TOPPINGS

## INGREDIENTS

- 1 head cauliflower, grated or processed into rice
- 1/2 cup shredded mozzarella cheese
- 1/4 cup grated Parmesan cheese
- 1 egg
- 1 teaspoon Italian seasoning
- Salt and pepper to taste

## PREPARATION

1. Preheat oven to 425°F (220°C) and line a baking sheet with parchment paper.
2. Steam the grated cauliflower in the microwave or on the stovetop until tender. Let it cool.
3. Place the cooled cauliflower in a clean kitchen towel and squeeze out excess moisture.
4. In a bowl, combine cauliflower, mozzarella, Parmesan, egg, Italian seasoning, salt, and pepper. Mix well.
5. Spread the cauliflower mixture onto the prepared baking sheet, shaping it into a round pizza crust.
6. Bake for 20-25 minutes or until the crust is golden brown and firm.

# ALMOND-CRUSTED BAKED CHICKEN TENDERS

## INGREDIENTS

- 1 pound chicken tenders
- 1 cup almond flour
- 1 teaspoon paprika
- 1/2 teaspoon garlic powder
- Salt and pepper to taste
- 2 eggs, beaten
- Cooking spray or olive oil

## PREPARATION

1. Preheat oven to 400°F (200°C) and line a baking sheet with parchment paper.
2. In a bowl, mix almond flour, paprika, garlic powder, salt, and pepper.
3. Dip each chicken tender into beaten eggs, then coat with the almond flour mixture.
4. Place the coated chicken tenders on the prepared baking sheet.
5. Lightly spray the tenders with cooking spray or drizzle with olive oil.
6. Bake for 20-25 minutes, turning halfway through, until the chicken is cooked through and golden.

# GREEN BEANS WITH TOASTED ALMONDS

## INGREDIENTS

- 1 pound green beans, trimmed
- 2 tablespoons olive oil
- 1/4 cup sliced almonds
- Salt and pepper to taste
- Lemon wedges for garnish (optional)

## PREPARATION

1. Blanch the green beans in boiling water for 2-3 minutes, then drain and rinse with cold water to stop cooking.
2. Heat olive oil in a skillet over medium heat. Add sliced almonds and toast until golden and fragrant.
3. Add blanched green beans to the skillet and sauté for a few minutes until heated through.
4. Season with salt and pepper.
5. Serve hot, garnished with lemon wedges if desired.

# EGGPLANT AND TOMATO CAPONATA

## INGREDIENTS

- 1 large eggplant, diced
- 2 tablespoons olive oil
- 1 onion, diced
- 2 cloves garlic, minced
- 1 can (14 oz) diced tomatoes
- 1/4 cup red wine vinegar
- 2 tablespoons capers, drained
- 2 tablespoons chopped fresh basil
- Salt and pepper to taste

## PREPARATION

1. Heat olive oil in a skillet over medium heat. Add diced eggplant and sauté until golden and softened. Remove and set aside.
2. In the same skillet, add diced onion and minced garlic. Sauté until onions are translucent.
3. Add diced tomatoes, red wine vinegar, capers, and cooked eggplant back to the skillet. Stir to combine.
4. Simmer the mixture for 10-15 minutes until it thickens.
5. Stir in chopped fresh basil. Season with salt and pepper.
6. Serve warm or cold as a dip or side dish.

# TUNA SALAD LETTUCE WRAPS

## INGREDIENTS

- 2 cans (5 oz each) tuna, drained
- 1/4 cup Greek yogurt (or mayonnaise)
- 1 stalk celery, finely chopped
- 1/4 cup red onion, finely chopped
- 1 tablespoon lemon juice
- 1 teaspoon Dijon mustard
- Salt and pepper to taste
- Lettuce leaves for wrapping

## PREPARATION

1. In a bowl, combine drained tuna, Greek yogurt (or mayonnaise), chopped celery, chopped red onion, lemon juice, Dijon mustard, salt, and pepper.
2. Mix until well combined.
3. Spoon the tuna salad onto lettuce leaves and wrap to form lettuce wraps.
4. Serve immediately as a light and refreshing meal.

# ROASTED BRUSSELS SPROUTS WITH BALSAMIC GLAZE

## INGREDIENTS

- 1 pound Brussels sprouts, trimmed and halved
- 2 tablespoons olive oil
- Salt and pepper to taste
- 2 tablespoons balsamic glaze

## PREPARATION

1. Preheat the oven to 400°F (200°C).
2. Toss Brussels sprouts with olive oil, salt, and pepper on a baking sheet.
3. Roast in the oven for 20-25 minutes until they are tender and golden brown.
4. Drizzle with balsamic glaze before serving.

# STUFFED CABBAGE ROLLS WITH LEAN BEEF AND BROWN RICE

## INGREDIENTS

- 1 large head of cabbage
- 1 pound lean ground beef
- 1 cup cooked brown rice
- 1 onion, finely chopped
- 2 cloves garlic, minced
- 1 can (15 oz) tomato sauce
- Salt and pepper to taste
- 1 teaspoon paprika
- 1 teaspoon dried oregano
- 1 teaspoon dried thyme

## PREPARATION

1. Preheat oven to 375°F (190°C).
2. Remove cabbage leaves, blanch them in boiling water until soft, then set aside.
3. In a skillet, cook ground beef with onion and garlic until browned. Drain excess fat.
4. Stir in cooked rice, half of the tomato sauce, and season with salt, pepper, paprika, oregano, and thyme.
5. Spoon beef mixture onto cabbage leaves, roll them up, and place seam-side down in a baking dish.
6. Pour remaining tomato sauce over the rolls, cover with foil, and bake for 40-45 minutes.

# HERBED BAKED COD WITH LEMON

## INGREDIENTS

- 4 cod fillets
- 2 tablespoons olive oil
- 2 cloves garlic, minced
- 1 tablespoon chopped fresh parsley
- 1 tablespoon chopped fresh dill
- Zest and juice of 1 lemon
- Salt and pepper to taste

## PREPARATION

1. Preheat oven to 375°F (190°C).
2. Place cod fillets on a baking dish lined with parchment paper.
3. In a small bowl, mix olive oil, garlic, parsley, dill, lemon zest, lemon juice, salt, and pepper.
4. Brush the herb mixture over the cod fillets.
5. Bake for 15-20 minutes or until fish is cooked through and flakes easily with a fork.

# SPAGHETTI SQUASH WITH MARINARA SAUCE

## INGREDIENTS

- 1 medium spaghetti squash
- 2 cups marinara sauce (homemade or store-bought)
- 1 tablespoon olive oil
- Salt and pepper to taste
- Fresh basil for garnish (optional)

## PREPARATION

1. Preheat oven to 400°F (200°C).
2. Cut the spaghetti squash in half lengthwise and remove seeds.
3. Drizzle olive oil over the squash halves, season with salt and pepper.
4. Place squash halves cut-side down on a baking sheet and bake for 30-40 minutes until tender.
5. Scrape the squash flesh with a fork to create spaghetti-like strands.
6. Heat marinara sauce in a saucepan and serve over the cooked spaghetti squash. Garnish with fresh basil if desired.

# CUCUMBER AND TOMATO SALAD WITH FETA

## INGREDIENTS

- 2 cucumbers, diced
- 2 cups cherry tomatoes, halved
- ½ cup crumbled feta cheese
- 2 tablespoons chopped fresh parsley
- 2 tablespoons olive oil
- 1 tablespoon red wine vinegar
- Salt and pepper to taste

## PREPARATION

1. In a bowl, combine cucumbers, cherry tomatoes, feta cheese, and parsley.
2. In a separate small bowl, whisk together olive oil, red wine vinegar, salt, and pepper.
3. Drizzle the dressing over the salad and toss gently to combine. Serve chilled.

# BROCCOLI AND CHEESE STUFFED CHICKEN BREAST

## INGREDIENTS

- 4 boneless, skinless chicken breasts
- 2 cups steamed broccoli florets, chopped
- 1 cup shredded cheddar cheese
- 2 cloves garlic, minced
- Salt and pepper to taste
- 1 tablespoon olive oil
- 1 teaspoon paprika

## PREPARATION

1. Preheat oven to 375°F (190°C).
2. Cut a pocket into each chicken breast without cutting all the way through.
3. In a bowl, mix chopped broccoli, shredded cheddar, garlic, salt, and pepper.
4. Stuff each chicken breast with the broccoli and cheese mixture, then secure with toothpicks.
5. Heat olive oil in an oven-safe skillet over medium-high heat.
6. Sear chicken breasts for 2-3 minutes per side until golden brown.
7. Sprinkle paprika over the chicken, then transfer the skillet to the oven and bake for 20-25 minutes or until chicken is cooked through.

# MOROCCAN-STYLE CHICKPEA STEW

## INGREDIENTS

- 2 tablespoons olive oil
- 1 onion, diced
- 2 cloves garlic, minced
- 1 teaspoon ground cumin
- 1 teaspoon ground coriander
- 1 teaspoon smoked paprika
- 1 can (15 oz) chickpeas, drained and rinsed
- 1 can (14 oz) diced tomatoes
- 2 cups vegetable broth
- 1 cup diced carrots
- 1 cup diced bell peppers (red and green)
- Salt and pepper to taste
- Fresh cilantro for garnish

## PREPARATION

1. Heat olive oil in a large pot over medium heat.
2. Sauté onions and garlic until softened.
3. Stir in cumin, coriander, and paprika, cook for another minute.
4. Add chickpeas, diced tomatoes, vegetable broth, carrots, and bell peppers.
5. Season with salt and pepper, bring to a simmer, and cook for 20-25 minutes until vegetables are tender.
6. Garnish with fresh cilantro before serving.

# BAKED APPLES WITH CINNAMON AND WALNUTS

## INGREDIENTS

- 4 apples (such as Granny Smith or Honeycrisp)
- ¼ cup chopped walnuts
- 2 tablespoons honey or maple syrup
- 1 teaspoon ground cinnamon
- 1 tablespoon unsalted butter (optional)

## PREPARATION

1. Preheat oven to 375°F (190°C).
2. Core the apples and place them in a baking dish.
3. In a bowl, mix chopped walnuts, honey (or maple syrup), and cinnamon.
4. Stuff the center of each apple with the walnut mixture. Top each with a small piece of butter (if using).
5. Bake for 25-30 minutes until apples are tender and slightly golden.

# GREEK CHICKEN SOUVLAKI SKEWERS

## INGREDIENTS

- 1 pound boneless, skinless chicken breast, cut into cubes
- ¼ cup olive oil
- 2 tablespoons lemon juice
- 2 cloves garlic, minced
- 1 teaspoon dried oregano
- Salt and pepper to taste
- Cherry tomatoes and red onion chunks for skewering

## PREPARATION

1. In a bowl, combine olive oil, lemon juice, minced garlic, dried oregano, salt, and pepper.
2. Marinate chicken cubes in the mixture for at least 30 minutes (or overnight) in the fridge.
3. Preheat grill or grill pan over medium-high heat.
4. Thread marinated chicken cubes onto skewers, alternating with cherry tomatoes and red onion chunks.
5. Grill skewers for about 6-8 minutes, turning occasionally until chicken is cooked through.

# BERRY CHIA SEED PUDDING

## INGREDIENTS

- ½ cup chia seeds
- 2 cups unsweetened almond milk (or any preferred milk)
- 1 tablespoon honey or maple syrup
- 1 teaspoon vanilla extract
- Mixed berries for topping

## PREPARATION

1. In a bowl, mix chia seeds, almond milk, honey (or maple syrup), and vanilla extract.
2. Let the mixture sit for 5 minutes, then whisk again to prevent clumps.
3. Refrigerate the mixture for at least 2 hours or overnight, stirring occasionally until it thickens into a pudding-like consistency.
4. Serve topped with fresh mixed berries.

# SMOOTHIES

# BERRY BLAST SMOOTHIE

## INGREDIENTS

- 1 cup mixed berries (strawberries, blueberries, raspberries)
- 1 ripe banana
- 1/2 cup Greek yogurt
- 1/2 cup almond milk (unsweetened)
- 1 tablespoon honey or maple syrup (optional)

## PREPARATION

1. Add all ingredients to a blender.
2. Blend until smooth and creamy.
3. Adjust sweetness with honey or maple syrup if desired.
4. Serve immediately.

# GREEN POWER SMOOTHIE

## INGREDIENTS

- 2 cups spinach leaves
- 1 ripe banana
- 1/2 avocado
- 1 tablespoon chia seeds
- 1 cup coconut water

## PREPARATION

1. Combine all ingredients in a blender.
2. Blend until well combined and smooth.
3. Add more coconut water if needed for desired consistency.
4. Pour into a glass and enjoy!

# TROPICAL PARADISE SMOOTHIE

## INGREDIENTS

- 1 cup frozen mango chunks
- 1/2 cup pineapple chunks
- 1/2 cup coconut milk
- 1/2 cup orange juice
- 1 tablespoon shredded coconut (optional)

## PREPARATION

1. Place all ingredients in a blender.
2. Blend until smooth.
3. Sprinkle shredded coconut on top if desired.
4. Serve chilled.

# CHOCOLATE BANANA PROTEIN SMOOTHIE

## INGREDIENTS

- 1 ripe banana
- 1 tablespoon cocoa powder
- 1/2 cup Greek yogurt
- 1 scoop chocolate protein powder
- 1 cup almond milk (unsweetened)

## PREPARATION

1. Combine all ingredients in a blender.
2. Blend until smooth and creamy.
3. Adjust consistency by adding more almond milk if needed.
4. Enjoy as a delicious protein-packed treat!

# MANGO GINGER SMOOTHIE

## INGREDIENTS

- 1 cup frozen mango chunks
- 1/2 inch fresh ginger (peeled and grated)
- 1/2 cup Greek yogurt
- 1 tablespoon honey
- 1/2 cup coconut water

## PREPARATION

1. Add all ingredients to a blender.
2. Blend until smooth and ginger is well incorporated.
3. Taste and add more honey if desired.
4. Pour into a glass and serve.

# SPINACH AND PINEAPPLE SMOOTHIE

## INGREDIENTS

- 2 cups fresh spinach leaves
- 1 cup pineapple chunks
- 1 ripe banana
- 1/2 cup coconut water or water
- 1/2 cup Greek yogurt

## PREPARATION

1. Combine spinach, pineapple, banana, and Greek yogurt in a blender.
2. Add coconut water or water to facilitate blending.
3. Blend until smooth and creamy.
4. Pour into glasses and enjoy!

# BLUEBERRY ALMOND SMOOTHIE

## INGREDIENTS

- 1 cup blueberries (fresh or frozen)
- 1/4 cup almonds (soaked overnight or use almond butter)
- 1/2 cup Greek yogurt
- 1 cup almond milk (unsweetened)

## PREPARATION

1. Place blueberries, soaked almonds or almond butter, Greek yogurt, and almond milk in a blender.
2. Blend until smooth and well combined.
3. Pour into glasses and savor the goodness!

# SPINACH AND PINEAPPLE SMOOTHIE

## INGREDIENTS

- 2 cups kale leaves (stems removed)
- 2 kiwi fruits (peeled and sliced)
- 1 ripe banana
- 1/2 cup coconut water
- 1 tablespoon honey (optional)

## PREPARATION

1. Add kale, kiwi, banana, coconut water, and honey (if using) to a blender.
2. Blend until smooth and the kale is well incorporated.
3. Adjust sweetness if needed.
4. Serve immediately.

# RASPBERRY COCONUT SMOOTHIE

## INGREDIENTS

- 1 cup raspberries (fresh or frozen)
- 1/2 cup coconut milk
- 1/2 cup Greek yogurt
- 1 tablespoon honey or maple syrup

## PREPARATION

1. Combine raspberries, coconut milk, Greek yogurt, and sweetener in a blender.
2. Blend until smooth and creamy.
3. Taste and add more honey or maple syrup if desired.
4. Pour into glasses and enjoy!

# APPLE CINNAMON SMOOTHIE

## INGREDIENTS

- 1 apple (cored and chopped)
- 1/2 teaspoon ground cinnamon
- 1/2 cup oats
- 1 cup almond milk (unsweetened)
- 1 tablespoon honey or maple syrup

## PREPARATION

1. Put chopped apple, ground cinnamon, oats, almond milk, and sweetener in a blender.
2. Blend until smooth and oats are well combined.
3. Adjust sweetness to taste.
4. Pour into glasses and savor the delightful flavors.

## STRAWBERRY SPINACH SMOOTHIE

### INGREDIENTS

- 1 cup fresh strawberries, hulled
- 1 ripe banana
- 1 cup fresh spinach leaves
- 1/2 cup Greek yogurt
- 1/2 cup almond milk (or preferred milk)
- 1 tablespoon honey or maple syrup (optional)
- Ice cubes (as desired)

### PREPARATION

1. Add strawberries, banana, spinach, Greek yogurt, almond milk, and honey (if using) to a blender.
2. Blend until smooth.
3. Add ice cubes and blend again until desired consistency is reached.
4. Pour into glasses and serve immediately.

## ORANGE CARROT GINGER SMOOTHIE

### INGREDIENTS

- 2 medium oranges, peeled and segmented
- 1 cup chopped carrots
- 1-inch piece fresh ginger, peeled and grated
- 1/2 cup coconut water (or regular water)
- 1 tablespoon chia seeds (optional)
- Ice cubes (as desired)

### PREPARATION

1. Place oranges, chopped carrots, grated ginger, coconut water, and chia seeds (if using) in a blender.
2. Blend until smooth.
3. Add ice cubes and blend again until desired consistency.
4. Pour into glasses and serve immediately.

## MIXED BERRY GREEK YOGURT SMOOTHIE

### INGREDIENTS

- 1 cup mixed berries (strawberries, blueberries, raspberries)
- 1/2 cup Greek yogurt
- 1 ripe banana
- 1/2 cup almond milk (or preferred milk)
- 1 tablespoon honey or maple syrup (optional)
- Ice cubes (as desired)

### PREPARATION

1. Combine mixed berries, Greek yogurt, banana, almond milk, and honey (if using) in a blender.
2. Blend until smooth.
3. Add ice cubes and blend again until desired texture is achieved.
4. Pour into glasses and serve immediately.

## AVOCADO BANANA SMOOTHIE

### INGREDIENTS

- 1 ripe avocado, peeled and pitted
- 1 ripe banana
- 1 cup spinach leaves
- 1 cup almond milk (or preferred milk)
- 1 tablespoon honey or maple syrup (optional)
- Ice cubes (as desired)

### PREPARATION

1. Place avocado, banana, spinach, almond milk, and honey (if using) into a blender.
2. Blend until smooth.
3. Add ice cubes and blend again for desired consistency.
4. Pour into glasses and serve immediately.

## POMEGRANATE BERRY SMOOTHIE

### INGREDIENTS

- 1/2 cup pomegranate seeds
- 1/2 cup mixed berries (blueberries, raspberries)
- 1/2 cup plain Greek yogurt
- 1/2 cup almond milk (or preferred milk)
- 1 tablespoon honey or maple syrup (optional)
- Ice cubes (as desired)

### PREPARATION

1. Combine pomegranate seeds, mixed berries, Greek yogurt, almond milk, and honey (if using) in a blender.
2. Blend until smooth.
3. Add ice cubes and blend again until desired consistency.
4. Pour into glasses and serve immediately.

## PAPAYA LIME SMOOTHIE

### INGREDIENTS

- 1 cup ripe papaya, peeled and seeded
- Juice of 1 lime
- 1/2 cup coconut water (or regular water)
- 1 tablespoon honey or maple syrup (optional)
- Ice cubes (as desired)

### PREPARATION

1. Place ripe papaya, lime juice, coconut water, and honey (if using) into a blender.
2. Blend until smooth.
3. Add ice cubes and blend again until desired texture.
4. Pour into glasses and serve immediately.

# PEACH AND OAT SMOOTHIE

## INGREDIENTS

- 1 cup sliced peaches (fresh or frozen)
- 1/2 cup rolled oats
- 1/2 cup Greek yogurt
- 1/2 cup almond milk (or preferred milk)
- 1 tablespoon honey or maple syrup (optional)
- Ice cubes (as desired)

## PREPARATION

1. Combine sliced peaches, rolled oats, Greek yogurt, almond milk, and honey (if using) in a blender.
2. Blend until smooth.
3. Add ice cubes and blend again until desired consistency.
4. Pour into glasses and serve immediately.

# WATERMELON MINT SMOOTHIE

## INGREDIENTS

- 2 cups cubed watermelon (seedless)
- 1/4 cup fresh mint leaves
- Juice of 1 lime
- 1/2 cup coconut water (or regular water)
- Ice cubes (as desired)

## PREPARATION

1. Place cubed watermelon, fresh mint leaves, lime juice, and coconut water into a blender.
2. Blend until smooth.
3. Add ice cubes and blend again until desired texture.
4. Pour into glasses and serve immediately.

# CHERRY ALMOND BUTTER SMOOTHIE

## INGREDIENTS

- 1 cup pitted cherries (fresh or frozen)
- 2 tablespoons almond butter
- 1/2 cup Greek yogurt
- 1/2 cup almond milk (or preferred milk)
- 1 tablespoon honey or maple syrup (optional)
- Ice cubes (as desired)

## PREPARATION

1. Combine pitted cherries, almond butter, Greek yogurt, almond milk, and honey (if using) in a blender.
2. Blend until smooth.
3. Add ice cubes and blend again for desired consistency.
4. Pour into glasses and serve immediately.

# SPINACH AND MANGO SMOOTHIE

## INGREDIENTS

- 1 cup fresh spinach leaves
- 1 ripe mango, peeled and diced
- 1/2 cup Greek yogurt
- 1/2 cup almond milk (or preferred milk)
- 1 tablespoon honey or maple syrup (optional)
- Ice cubes (as desired)

## PREPARATION

1. Place spinach leaves, diced mango, Greek yogurt, almond milk, and honey (if using) into a blender.
2. Blend until smooth.
3. Add ice cubes and blend again until desired texture.
4. Pour into glasses and serve immediately.

# CRANBERRY WALNUT SMOOTHIE

## INGREDIENTS

- 1 cup cranberries (fresh or frozen)
- 1 ripe banana
- 1/2 cup Greek yogurt
- 1/4 cup walnuts
- 1 cup almond milk (unsweetened)
- Honey or sweetener (optional, to taste)
- Ice cubes (optional)

## PREPARATION

1. Place cranberries, banana, Greek yogurt, walnuts, and almond milk in a blender.
2. Blend until smooth and creamy.
3. Taste and add honey or sweetener if desired.
4. Add ice cubes and blend again for a colder consistency (if preferred).
5. Pour into glasses and serve.

# PINEAPPLE TURMERIC SMOOTHIE

## INGREDIENTS

- 1 cup pineapple chunks (fresh or frozen)
- 1/2 teaspoon turmeric powder
- 1/2 cup coconut milk
- 1/2 cup plain yogurt
- 1 tablespoon honey or maple syrup (optional, to taste)
- Ice cubes (optional)

## PREPARATION

1. Combine pineapple chunks, turmeric powder, coconut milk, plain yogurt, and sweetener (if using) in a blender.
2. Blend until smooth.
3. Add ice cubes if desired for a colder texture and blend again.
4. Pour into glasses and serve.

# FIG AND HONEY SMOOTHIE

## INGREDIENTS

- 6-8 dried figs (soaked in water for 1-2 hours, then drained)
- 1 cup unsweetened almond milk
- 1/2 cup Greek yogurt
- 1 tablespoon honey
- Pinch of cinnamon (optional)
- Ice cubes (optional)

## PREPARATION

1. Place soaked figs, almond milk, Greek yogurt, honey, and cinnamon (if using) in a blender.
2. Blend until the mixture becomes smooth.
3. Add ice cubes for a colder consistency if desired and blend briefly.
4. Pour into glasses and serve.

# CANTALOUPE BASIL SMOOTHIE

## INGREDIENTS

- 2 cups cubed cantaloupe
- 1/4 cup fresh basil leaves
- 1/2 cup coconut water
- 1/2 cup plain yogurt
- 1 tablespoon lime juice
- Honey or sweetener (optional, to taste)
- Ice cubes (optional)

## PREPARATION

1. Combine cantaloupe, basil leaves, coconut water, plain yogurt, lime juice, and sweetener (if using) in a blender.
2. Blend until smooth.
3. Add ice cubes if desired for a chilled drink and blend briefly.
4. Pour into glasses, garnish with basil leaves if desired, and serve.

## BLACKBERRY CHIA SEED SMOOTHIE

### INGREDIENTS

- 1 cup blackberries (fresh or frozen)
- 1 tablespoon chia seeds
- 1/2 cup spinach leaves
- 1/2 cup almond milk (unsweetened)
- 1/2 cup plain Greek yogurt
- Honey or sweetener (optional, to taste)
- Ice cubes (optional)

### PREPARATION

1. Combine blackberries, chia seeds, spinach leaves, almond milk, Greek yogurt, and sweetener (if using) in a blender.
2. Blend until smooth.
3. Add ice cubes if desired and blend again for a colder texture.
4. Pour into glasses and serve.

## PEAR GINGER GREEN SMOOTHIE

### INGREDIENTS

- 1 ripe pear, cored and chopped
- 1 cup spinach or kale leaves
- 1-inch piece fresh ginger, peeled and grated
- 1/2 cup coconut water
- 1/2 cup plain yogurt
- 1 tablespoon honey or maple syrup (optional)
- Ice cubes (optional)

### PREPARATION

1. Combine chopped pear, spinach or kale leaves, grated ginger, coconut water, plain yogurt, and sweetener (if using) in a blender.
2. Blend until thoroughly mixed and smooth.
3. Add ice cubes for a colder consistency, if desired, and blend briefly.
4. Pour into glasses and serve.

# PLUM VANILLA SMOOTHIE

## INGREDIENTS

- 2 ripe plums, pitted and sliced
- 1/2 cup unsweetened almond milk
- 1/2 cup Greek yogurt
- 1/2 teaspoon vanilla extract
- 1 tablespoon honey or maple syrup (optional)
- Ice cubes (optional)

## PREPARATION

1. Combine sliced plums, almond milk, Greek yogurt, vanilla extract, and sweetener (if using) in a blender.
2. Blend until smooth and creamy.
3. Add ice cubes if desired for a cooler drink and blend briefly.
4. Pour into glasses and serve.

# BLUEBERRY AVOCADO SMOOTHIE

## INGREDIENTS

- 1 cup blueberries (fresh or frozen)
- 1/2 ripe avocado
- 1/2 cup spinach leaves
- 1 cup almond milk (unsweetened)
- 1 tablespoon honey or maple syrup (optional)
- Ice cubes (optional)

## PREPARATION

1. Combine blueberries, ripe avocado, spinach leaves, almond milk, and sweetener (if using) in a blender.
2. Blend until thoroughly combined and smooth.
3. Add ice cubes for a colder consistency if preferred, and blend briefly.
4. Pour into glasses and serve.

# PUMPKIN PIE SMOOTHIE

## INGREDIENTS

- 1/2 cup canned pumpkin puree
- 1 ripe banana
- 1/2 teaspoon pumpkin pie spice
- 1 cup unsweetened almond milk
- 1/2 cup plain Greek yogurt
- Honey or sweetener (optional, to taste)
- Ice cubes (optional)

## PREPARATION

1. Combine pumpkin puree, ripe banana, pumpkin pie spice, almond milk, Greek yogurt, and sweetener (if using) in a blender.
2. Blend until smooth and well mixed.
3. Add ice cubes if desired for a chilled texture, and blend briefly.
4. Pour into glasses, sprinkle extra pumpkin pie spice on top if desired, and serve.

# HONEYDEW MINT SMOOTHIE

## INGREDIENTS

- 2 cups diced honeydew melon
- 1/4 cup fresh mint leaves
- 1/2 cup coconut water
- 1/2 cup plain yogurt
- 1 tablespoon honey or maple syrup (optional)
- Ice cubes (optional)

## PREPARATION

1. Combine diced honeydew melon, fresh mint leaves, coconut water, plain yogurt, and sweetener (if using) in a blender.
2. Blend until smooth and mint is well incorporated.
3. Add ice cubes for a cooler drink, if desired, and blend briefly.
4. Pour into glasses, garnish with mint leaves, and serve.

## MIXED BERRIES AND GREEK YOGURT PROTEIN SMOOTHIE

### INGREDIENTS

- 1 cup mixed berries (strawberries, blueberries, raspberries)
- 1/2 cup Greek yogurt
- 1/2 cup almond milk (or any preferred milk)
- 1 tablespoon honey or maple syrup (optional)
- Ice cubes (optional)

### PREPARATION

1. Place mixed berries, Greek yogurt, almond milk, and sweetener (if using) into a blender.
2. Blend until smooth and creamy.
3. Add ice cubes if desired and blend again until well combined.
4. Pour into a glass and enjoy!

## BEETROOT AND BERRY SMOOTHIE

### INGREDIENTS

- 1 small cooked beetroot, peeled and chopped
- 1/2 cup mixed berries (strawberries, raspberries)
- 1/2 cup plain Greek yogurt
- 1/2 cup coconut water or water
- 1 tablespoon honey or agave syrup (optional)

### PREPARATION

1. In a blender, combine the cooked beetroot, mixed berries, Greek yogurt, coconut water (or water), and sweetener if desired.
2. Blend until smooth and well combined.
3. Pour into a glass and serve fresh.

# CHERRY COCOA SMOOTHIE

## INGREDIENTS

- 1 cup frozen cherries
- 1 tablespoon unsweetened cocoa powder
- 1/2 cup almond milk (or any preferred milk)
- 1/2 cup plain Greek yogurt
- 1 tablespoon honey or maple syrup (optional)

## PREPARATION

1. Place frozen cherries, cocoa powder, almond milk, Greek yogurt, and sweetener (if using) into a blender.
2. Blend until smooth and creamy.
3. Adjust sweetness if needed by adding more honey or syrup.
4. Pour into a glass and enjoy the chocolaty goodness!

# APRICOT ALMOND SMOOTHIE

## INGREDIENTS

- 1 cup apricots (fresh or frozen)
- 1/4 cup almonds
- 1/2 cup almond milk (or any preferred milk)
- 1/2 cup plain Greek yogurt
- 1 tablespoon honey or agave syrup (optional)

## PREPARATION

1. Combine apricots, almonds, almond milk, Greek yogurt, and sweetener (if using) in a blender.
2. Blend until smooth and creamy.
3. Taste and adjust sweetness if necessary.
4. Pour into a glass and enjoy the delightful apricot-almond flavor.

# LEMON RASPBERRY SMOOTHIE

## INGREDIENTS

- 1 cup raspberries (fresh or frozen)
- Juice of 1 lemon
- Zest of 1 lemon
- 1/2 cup plain Greek yogurt
- 1/2 cup almond milk (or any preferred milk)
- 1 tablespoon honey or agave syrup (optional)

## PREPARATION

1. In a blender, combine raspberries, lemon juice, lemon zest, Greek yogurt, almond milk, and sweetener if desired.
2. Blend until smooth and creamy.
3. Taste and adjust sweetness if needed.
4. Pour into a glass and enjoy the refreshing tang of lemon and raspberry.

# CARROT CAKE SMOOTHIE

## INGREDIENTS

- 1 cup shredded carrots
- 1/2 banana
- 1/4 cup rolled oats
- 1/2 teaspoon ground cinnamon
- 1/2 cup plain Greek yogurt
- 1/2 cup almond milk (or any preferred milk)
- 1 tablespoon honey or maple syrup (optional)

## PREPARATION

1. Combine shredded carrots, banana, rolled oats, cinnamon, Greek yogurt, almond milk, and sweetener (if using) in a blender.
2. Blend until smooth and creamy.
3. Adjust sweetness or thickness by adding more honey or milk if desired.
4. Pour into a glass and savor the flavors reminiscent of carrot cake.

## MANGO COCONUT CHIA SMOOTHIE

### INGREDIENTS

- 1 cup diced mango
- 1/2 cup coconut milk
- 1/2 cup plain Greek yogurt
- 1 tablespoon chia seeds
- 1 tablespoon honey or agave syrup (optional)

### PREPARATION

1. In a blender, combine diced mango, coconut milk, Greek yogurt, chia seeds, and sweetener if desired.
2. Blend until smooth and well combined.
3. Taste and adjust sweetness if necessary.
4. Pour into a glass and enjoy the tropical goodness.

## GREEN TEA BERRY SMOOTHIE

### INGREDIENTS

- 1 cup mixed berries (blueberries, strawberries)
- 1/2 cup brewed green tea, cooled
- 1/2 cup plain Greek yogurt
- 1 tablespoon honey or agave syrup (optional)

### PREPARATION

1. Combine mixed berries, brewed green tea, Greek yogurt, and sweetener (if using) in a blender.
2. Blend until smooth and well incorporated.
3. Adjust sweetness if needed.
4. Pour into a glass and enjoy the antioxidant-rich green tea blend.

## BANANA WALNUT PROTEIN SMOOTHIE

### INGREDIENTS

- 1 ripe banana
- 1/4 cup walnuts
- 1/2 cup almond milk (or any preferred milk)
- 1/2 cup plain Greek yogurt
- 1 tablespoon honey or maple syrup (optional)

### PREPARATION

1. In a blender, combine ripe banana, walnuts, almond milk, Greek yogurt, and sweetener (if using).
2. Blend until smooth and creamy.
3. Adjust sweetness if necessary.
4. Pour into a glass and relish the banana-walnut fusion.

## RASPBERRY PISTACHIO SMOOTHIE

### INGREDIENTS

- 1 cup raspberries (fresh or frozen)
- 1/4 cup shelled pistachios
- 1/2 cup almond milk (or any preferred milk)
- 1/2 cup plain Greek yogurt
- 1 tablespoon honey or agave syrup (optional)

### PREPARATION

1. Combine raspberries, pistachios, almond milk, Greek yogurt, and sweetener (if using) in a blender.
2. Blend until smooth and well combined.
3. Taste and adjust sweetness if necessary.
4. Pour into a glass and enjoy the delightful raspberry-pistachio blend.

# PINEAPPLE TURMERIC GINGER SMOOTHIE

## INGREDIENTS

- 1 cup frozen pineapple chunks
- 1 banana
- 1/2 teaspoon ground turmeric
- 1 teaspoon grated fresh ginger
- 1 cup unsweetened coconut or almond milk
- 1/2 cup Greek yogurt (optional)
- Honey or agave syrup (optional, to sweeten)

## PREPARATION

1. Add all ingredients to a blender.
2. Blend until smooth and creamy.
3. Taste and adjust sweetness if needed with honey or agave syrup.
4. Pour into a glass and enjoy!

# CUCUMBER MELON SMOOTHIE

## INGREDIENTS

- 1 cup chopped cucumber
- 1 cup chopped honeydew melon
- 1/2 cup plain Greek yogurt
- 1 tablespoon honey or agave syrup
- 1/2 cup coconut water or water
- Ice cubes (optional)

## PREPARATION

1. Combine all ingredients in a blender.
2. Blend until smooth.
3. Add ice cubes if desired for a chilled texture.
4. Pour into a glass and serve immediately.

# DATE AND ALMOND SMOOTHIE

## INGREDIENTS

- 2-3 pitted dates
- 1/4 cup almonds
- 1 banana
- 1 cup unsweetened almond milk
- 1/2 teaspoon vanilla extract
- Ice cubes (optional)

## PREPARATION

1. Soak the dates in warm water for a few minutes to soften.
2. Combine dates, almonds, banana, almond milk, and vanilla extract in a blender.
3. Blend until smooth.
4. Add ice cubes if desired for a colder consistency.
5. Pour into a glass and enjoy!

# BLUEBERRY FLAXSEED SMOOTHIE

## INGREDIENTS

- 1 cup frozen blueberries
- 1 tablespoon ground flaxseeds
- 1/2 cup plain Greek yogurt
- 1 cup unsweetened almond milk
- Honey or maple syrup (optional, to sweeten)
- Ice cubes (optional)

## PREPARATION

1. Place blueberries, flaxseeds, yogurt, almond milk, and sweetener (if using) into a blender.
2. Blend until smooth.
3. Add ice cubes for a frostier texture if desired.
4. Pour into a glass and serve immediately.

# APPLE KALE SPINACH SMOOTHIE

## INGREDIENTS

- 1 apple, cored and chopped
- Handful of kale leaves
- Handful of spinach leaves
- 1/2 frozen banana
- 1 cup unsweetened almond milk or water
- Dash of cinnamon (optional)
- Ice cubes (optional)

## PREPARATION

1. Combine apple, kale, spinach, banana, almond milk or water, and cinnamon in a blender.
2. Blend until smooth.
3. Add ice cubes if preferred.
4. Pour into a glass and enjoy the green goodness!

# DRAGON FRUIT PINEAPPLE SMOOTHIE

## INGREDIENTS

- 1 cup diced dragon fruit (pitaya), fresh or frozen
- 1 cup diced pineapple
- 1/2 cup coconut water or coconut milk
- Juice of 1 lime
- Ice cubes (optional)

## PREPARATION

1. Combine dragon fruit, pineapple, coconut water or milk, and lime juice in a blender.
2. Blend until smooth.
3. Add ice cubes for a colder texture, if desired.
4. Pour into a glass and savor the tropical flavors.

# RASPBERRY MINT SMOOTHIE

## INGREDIENTS

- 1 cup frozen raspberries
- Handful of fresh mint leaves
- 1/2 cup plain Greek yogurt
- 1 cup unsweetened almond milk
- Honey or agave syrup (optional, to sweeten)
- Ice cubes (optional)

## PREPARATION

1. Place raspberries, mint leaves, yogurt, almond milk, and sweetener (if using) in a blender.
2. Blend until smooth and mint leaves are finely blended.
3. Add ice cubes for a chillier drink, if desired.
4. Pour into a glass and relish the refreshing taste.

# PAPAYA COCONUT SMOOTHIE

## INGREDIENTS

- 1 cup diced ripe papaya
- 1/2 cup coconut milk
- 1/2 cup plain Greek yogurt
- 1 tablespoon honey or agave syrup
- Ice cubes (optional)

## PREPARATION

1. Combine papaya, coconut milk, yogurt, and sweetener in a blender.
2. Blend until creamy and well mixed.
3. Add ice cubes if you prefer a colder drink.
4. Pour into a glass and enjoy the tropical blend.

# ORANGE CREAMSICLE SMOOTHIE

## INGREDIENTS

- 1 large orange, peeled and segmented
- 1/2 cup plain Greek yogurt
- 1/2 cup unsweetened almond milk or orange juice
- 1 tablespoon honey or agave syrup
- Vanilla extract (optional)
- Ice cubes (optional)

## PREPARATION

1. Place orange segments, yogurt, almond milk or orange juice, sweetener, and a splash of vanilla extract in a blender.
2. Blend until smooth.
3. Add ice cubes for a frostier consistency.
4. Pour into a glass and relish the creamy orange delight.

# STRAWBERRY BASIL SMOOTHIE

## INGREDIENTS

- 1 cup fresh strawberries, hulled
- Handful of fresh basil leaves
- 1/2 cup plain Greek yogurt
- 1 cup unsweetened almond milk
- Honey or agave syrup (optional, to sweeten)
- Ice cubes (optional)

## PREPARATION

1. Combine strawberries, basil leaves, yogurt, almond milk, and sweetener (if using) in a blender.
2. Blend until smooth and basil is finely blended.
3. Add ice cubes for a chillier beverage.
4. Pour into a glass and enjoy the unique blend of flavors.

# CONCLUSION

The "Glucose Goddess Cookbook" is a light of hope and flavor, illuminating the road to healthy living for those looking for balance in their blood glucose levels. Its pages contain not just recipes, but also a path toward fitness and culinary joy, inspiring everyone to embrace a life full of tasty and wholesome meals.

This cookbook reveals the secrets of harmonizing flavors and nutrients with each meal, opening a world where health and taste dwell in perfect harmony. It's a monument to the power of healthful ingredients, helping people through the maze of maintaining blood glucose levels like a kind friend.

This cookbook is more than simply a compilation of culinary masterpieces; it is a promise of restored vigor and joy in eating. It enables people to retake control over their health without sacrificing the pleasure of delicious cuisine.

The cookbook's strength rests in its simplicity; it does not require sophisticated ingredients or intricate cooking processes. Instead, it highlights the splendor of nature's bounty—fresh fruits and vegetables, colorful veggies, lean meats, and healthy grains—all artfully weaved into meals that promote stable blood glucose levels.

Readers discover not just wonderful recipes but also a renewed confidence in controlling their health as they begin on their culinary adventure via the "Glucose Goddess Cookbook." It's a manual that encourages a lifestyle in which every meal becomes a pleasurable step toward wellbeing by creating a greater awareness of food's influence on well-being.

May this cookbook be a companion, encouraging and leading people on a path of wholesome enjoyment. Let it serve as a reminder that regulating blood glucose does not have to be a chore, but rather a pleasurable journey into the world of tempting tastes and increased well-being.

Made in the USA
Columbia, SC
08 March 2024

32835848R00037